I0824573

WHEN PAUL REVERE RODE

VOICES FROM THE FIRST NIGHT OF THE AMERICAN REVOLUTION

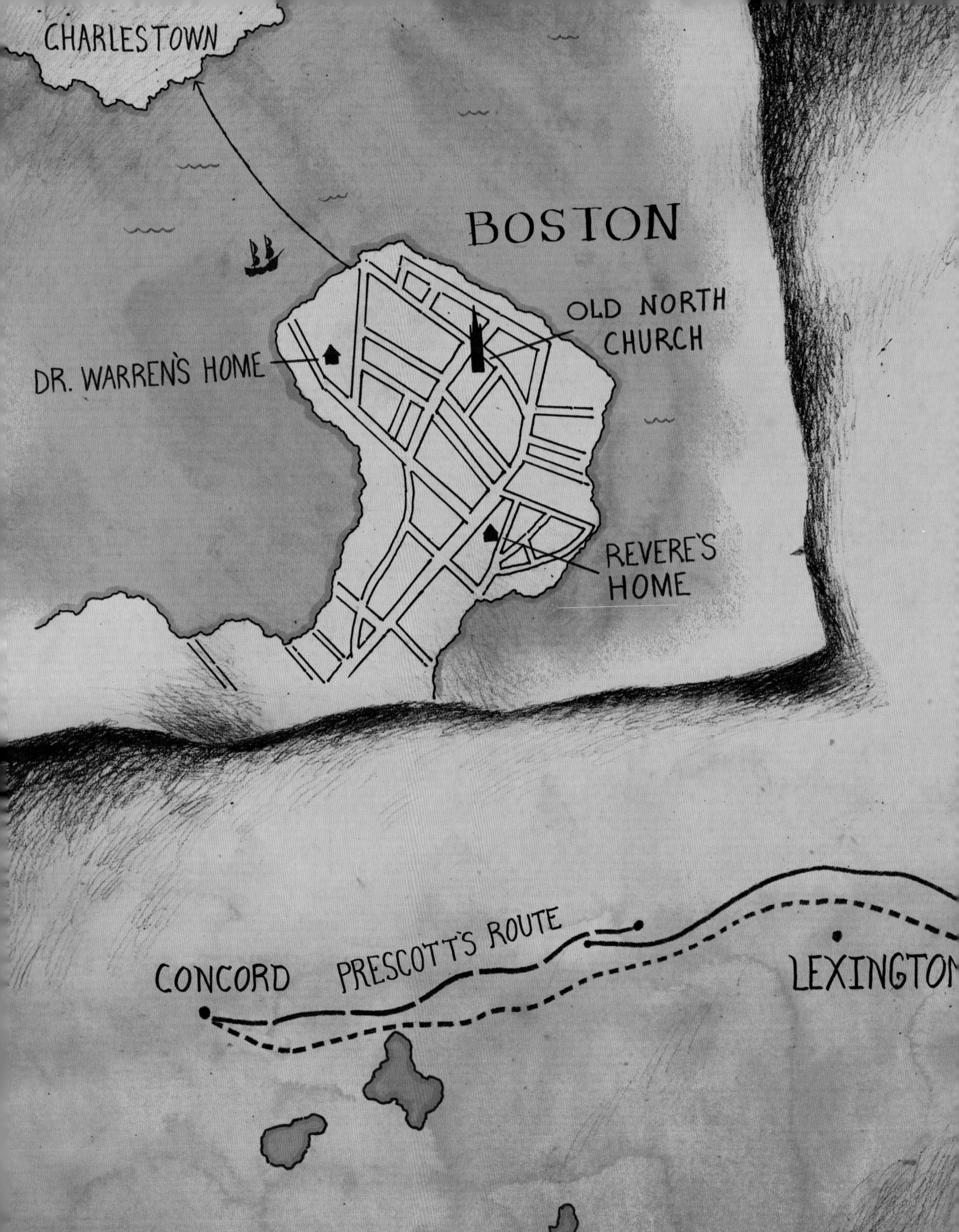
CHARLESTOWN
BOSTON
OLD NORTH CHURCH
DR. WARREN'S HOME
REVERE'S HOME
PRESCOTT'S ROUTE
CONCORD
LEXINGTON

REVERE'S ROUTE
BOSTON
BRITISH TROOPS

WHEN PAUL REVERE RODE

VOICES FROM THE FIRST NIGHT OF THE AMERICAN REVOLUTION

SARAH L. THOMSON

ILLUSTRATED BY

NIK HENDERSON

CALKINS CREEK

AN IMPRINT OF ASTRA BOOKS FOR YOUNG READERS

New York

During the 1760s and 1770s, some people in the thirteen American colonies were restless under the power of King George III of England. There were taxes (on things like paper, playing cards, and tea) that colonists did not get to vote on, but had to pay. There were rules that they had to provide supplies and living space for British soldiers. There was a street brawl known as the Boston Massacre that led to those soldiers firing on and killing colonists.

Some colonists began to speak up, demanding more of a voice in choosing their own leaders and making the laws they had to obey. Across Massachusetts, colonists gathered arms and ammunition, storing them secretly in case they needed to fight for their rights.

In April of 1775, people in Boston noticed that British troops—called the Regulars—had been more active than usual. Many suspected they were preparing for a mission to seize weapons hidden in the town of Concord. Perhaps they would even arrest leaders of the protests against British rule, men like John Hancock and Samuel Adams, who were staying out of sight in nearby Lexington.

"Every Act of Oppression will sour their Tempers . . . and hasten their final Revolt."

—Benjamin Franklin, letter, 1767

". . . one of the soldiers having received a severe blow with a stick, stepped a little on one side and instantly fired. . . ."

—Captain Thomas Preston, account of the Boston Massacre, 1770

"All might be free if they valued freedom, and defended it as they ought."

—Samuel Adams, *The Boston Gazette*, 1771

"Can any one reason be assigned why 160,000 electors in the island of Great Britain should give law to four millions in the states of America?"

—Thomas Jefferson, *A Summary View of the Rights of British America*, 1774

AFTERNOON OF APRIL 18, 1775

Paul Revere was a silversmith in Boston and a member of the Sons of Liberty, a secret group resisting rules, taxes, and laws they felt were unjust. One April afternoon, a stable boy heard news from a friend that he knew would greatly interest Revere.

The patter of hooves
like the roll of a drum
like the thump of a heart
like a fist on the door

A good horse will run
like speed is his soul
and wind is an enemy
he can defeat

That's how I run
through the alleys of Boston,
cobble and brick,
a track for my feet
to burst in the door
to be first with the news
for time is an enemy
speed can defeat:

The soldiers!
The Regulars!
They're on the march!

". . . you will march . . . with the utmost expedition and secrecy to Concord, where you will seize and destroy all the artillery, ammunition, provisions, tents, small arms and all military stores whatever."

—General Thomas Gage, royal governor of Massachusetts and commander of British forces in North America, 1775

AFTERNOON OR EVENING OF APRIL 18, 1775

Paul Revere's friend, Dr. Joseph Warren, knew someone (he never revealed who it was) keeping an eye on the movements of the troops in Boston. Warren asked this person if rumors of a British mission on the night of April 18th were true.

My face—forgotten.
My name—unmentioned.
My word a stone
dropped in a well—

Yes.

It's true.

It's time.

It's now.

The echoes
last for centuries.

"Be circumspect, vigilant, active, and brave."
—Dr. Joseph Warren, *The Boston Massacre Oration*, 1775

BETWEEN 10:00 AND 11:00 P.M., APRIL 18, 1775

After talking with Dr. Warren, Paul Revere got ready to ride to Lexington, where John Hancock and Samuel Adams were staying. He also asked two friends to climb the tower of the Old North Church with lanterns to flash a message. If Revere couldn't make it out of Boston, watchers in Charlestown would still know that British troops were leaving the city.

I've heard these bells ring
seen men dragged off their feet
by the pull of the rope
by the weight of the song.

But now each bell hangs
watchful and still—
muffled brass tongue
and a mouthful of night.

And no sound at all
soars out from the steeple—
but two burning lanterns
call out a warning:

Be careful
Be watchful
Beware and be brave

"... if the British went out by Water, we would shew two Lanthorns in the North Church Steeple ..."

—Paul Revere, letter, written around 1798

SOMETIME IN THE NIGHT, APRIL 18, 1775

Not every person in Boston supported Revere's mission. Many colonists remained loyal to England and were shocked and frightened to see friends and neighbors willing to take up arms against their king. One of those loyalists—also called Tories—was the rector, or priest, of Old North Church, Reverend Mather Byles Jr.

When did the first face in the pew
turn aside from mine?

When did a cup of tea
become a crime?

Why should crossing an ocean
change who and what I am?

How did *I* become the enemy?

"If any person from this time forward purchase or consume any tea, such person shall be looked upon as an enemy to this town and to this country."

—Reverend Jonas Clarke, public resolution passed by the town of Lexington to protest a new tax on tea, 1773

10:30 P.M., APRIL 18, 1775

Travel out of Boston had been forbidden, and anyone caught trying to leave the city would be arrested. Despite the danger, Joshua Bentley and Thomas Richardson agreed to row Paul Revere across the Charles River.

Can't help thinking the moon
is a Tory tonight,
loyal at heart to a far-off king,
round and gold as a crown.

Soon she'll rise above the rooftops,
snag and snare us
in chains of light,
end our journey before it begins.

But look—the moon loves liberty!
Like a sleeping child,
she rests her cheek
on the dark horizon

and the shadows she casts
melt into water,
melt right over us,

as we row past
the bulk of a warship
soft as shadow ourselves

to bump our bow
on a Charlestown dock
safe over the water at last.

"It was then young flood, the Ship was winding,
and the moon was Rising."
—Paul Revere, letter, written around 1798

11:00 P.M., APRIL 18, 1775

Paul Revere needed a horse to set off on his mission. Among his friends and allies on the Charlestown side of the river was John Larkin, who loaned him one—"a very good horse," so Revere later said.

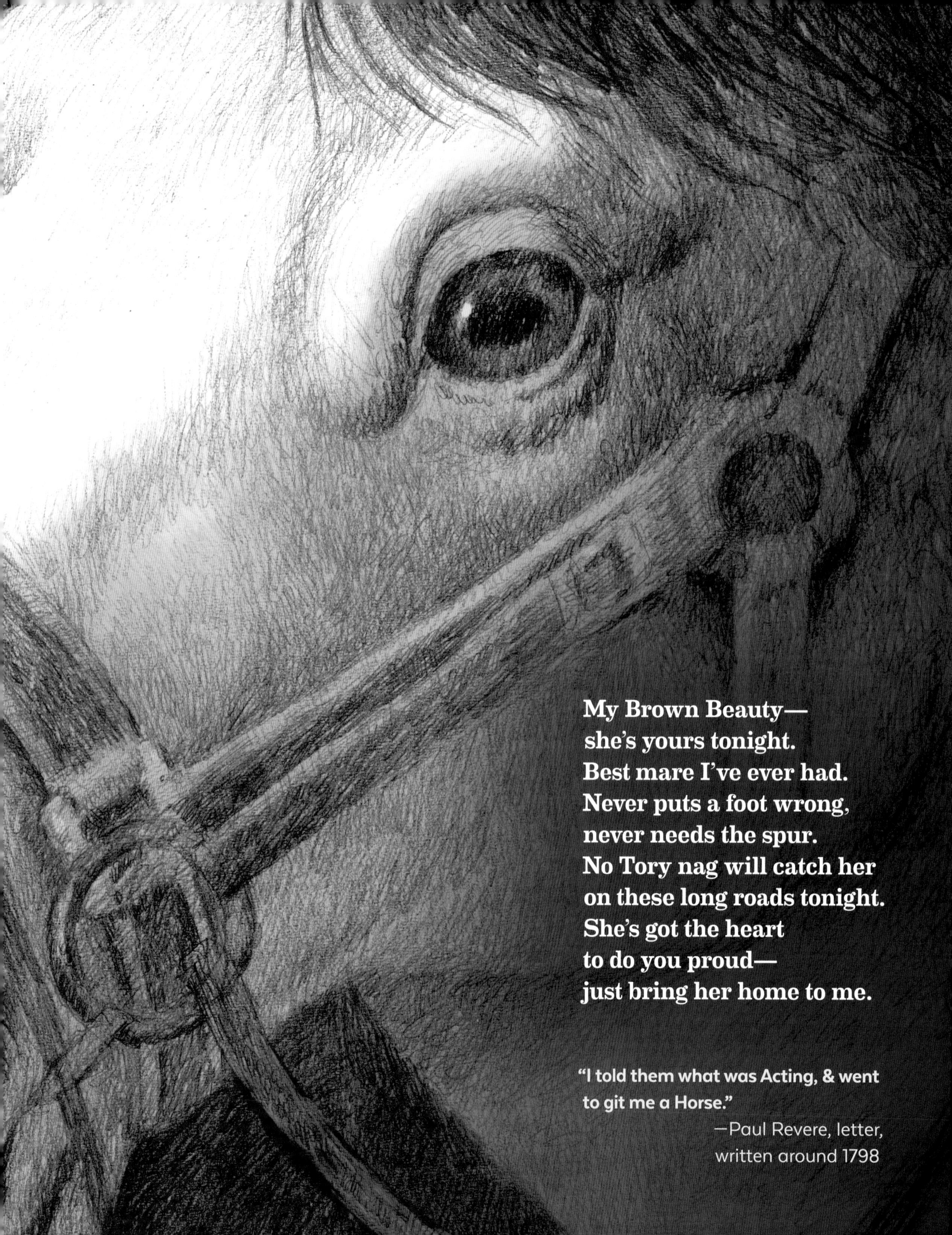

My Brown Beauty—
she's yours tonight.
Best mare I've ever had.
Never puts a foot wrong,
never needs the spur.
No Tory nag will catch her
on these long roads tonight.
She's got the heart
to do you proud—
just bring her home to me.

"I told them what was Acting, & went to git me a Horse."

—Paul Revere, letter,
written around 1798

BETWEEN 11:00 P.M. AND MIDNIGHT, APRIL 18, 1775

This night was not the first time Paul Revere had ridden to carry news and warnings to his fellow colonists. Did he have any sense that this particular ride would be the one history would remember?

Think of a musket—

set on the half cock
powder in the pan
bullet down the barrel

pull back the cock till it locks in place

wait
wait
wait

finger on the trigger

wait
wait
wait

till your shot will count

finger to trigger
flint to hammer
spark to powder
and your bullet will fly.

Tonight I'm the spark
but no way to know
where this bullet will fly

if this shot will count.

“The Spirit of Liberty was never higher than at present.”
—Paul Revere, letter, 1774

MIDNIGHT, BETWEEN APRIL 18 AND 19, 1775

After spreading his warning along the road, Revere reached the home of a minister, Jonas Clarke. John Hancock and Samuel Adams were staying there. The house was guarded by eight members of the Lexington Militia, including Sergeant William Munroe.

"About midnight, Col. Paul Revere rode up. . . ."
—Sergeant William Munroe, Lexington Militia, sworn statement, 1825

Spring leaves and tender grass
sigh and whisper
dove and owl coo and call
mice scratch and skitter

a silence made of tiny sounds
a night brimful of peace

till that rider comes storming
out of the dark,
poor mare thundering out her breath—

Hush that noise!
I tell him.
Folks are trying to sleep!

Noise!
he answers back.
You'll have noise enough before long!

I learned how right he was
before the next soft night came calling.

MIDNIGHT, BETWEEN APRIL 18 AND 19, 1775

Jonas Clarke had twelve children, and most were home the night Paul Revere and a second rider, William Dawes, arrived. Elizabeth, known as Betty, was eleven years old. She never forgot what she saw and did that night and the day after.

Mr. Hancock, he brought
a salmon for dinner
so fresh it could wiggle
right there on the plate.

Then bad news blew into
the house like a hurricane,
tumbled us all
into panic and packing and prayer.

Mr. Hancock rushed off
with his friend Mr. Adams
but sent the coach back—
there were three things he wanted:

Miss Dolly Quinsy
(he married her later)
his dear Aunt Hancock
(to keep it all proper)

and that salmon too!

"... the war began on the Common which I can now see from this window as I sit here writing, and can see, in my mind, just as plain, all the British troops marching off the Common to Concord. . . ."

—Betty Clarke, letter, 1841

AROUND 1:30 A.M., APRIL 19, 1775

Revere and Dawes left the Clarke home and headed northwest toward Concord. They met Doctor Samuel Prescott on his way home from visiting his fiancée. Since Prescott was known and trusted in the area, the two invited him to join their mission. But Dawes, Revere, and Prescott were not the only horsemen on the road that night.

The dark road unwinding
carries me from her—
her name in my heart
chimes like soft silver bells.

The dark road before me
brings me companions,
two men on a mission
they ask me to join.

The dark road holds perils—
armed soldiers who face us,
demanding surrender,
blocking our way.

But I know this dark road
better than any
and set my horse springing
across a stone wall.

The dark road will sweep me
fast into the future,
the only one left
to carry the warning!

"We were overtaken by a young Docter Prescot, whom we found to be a high Son of Liberty."

—Paul Revere, letter, written around 1798

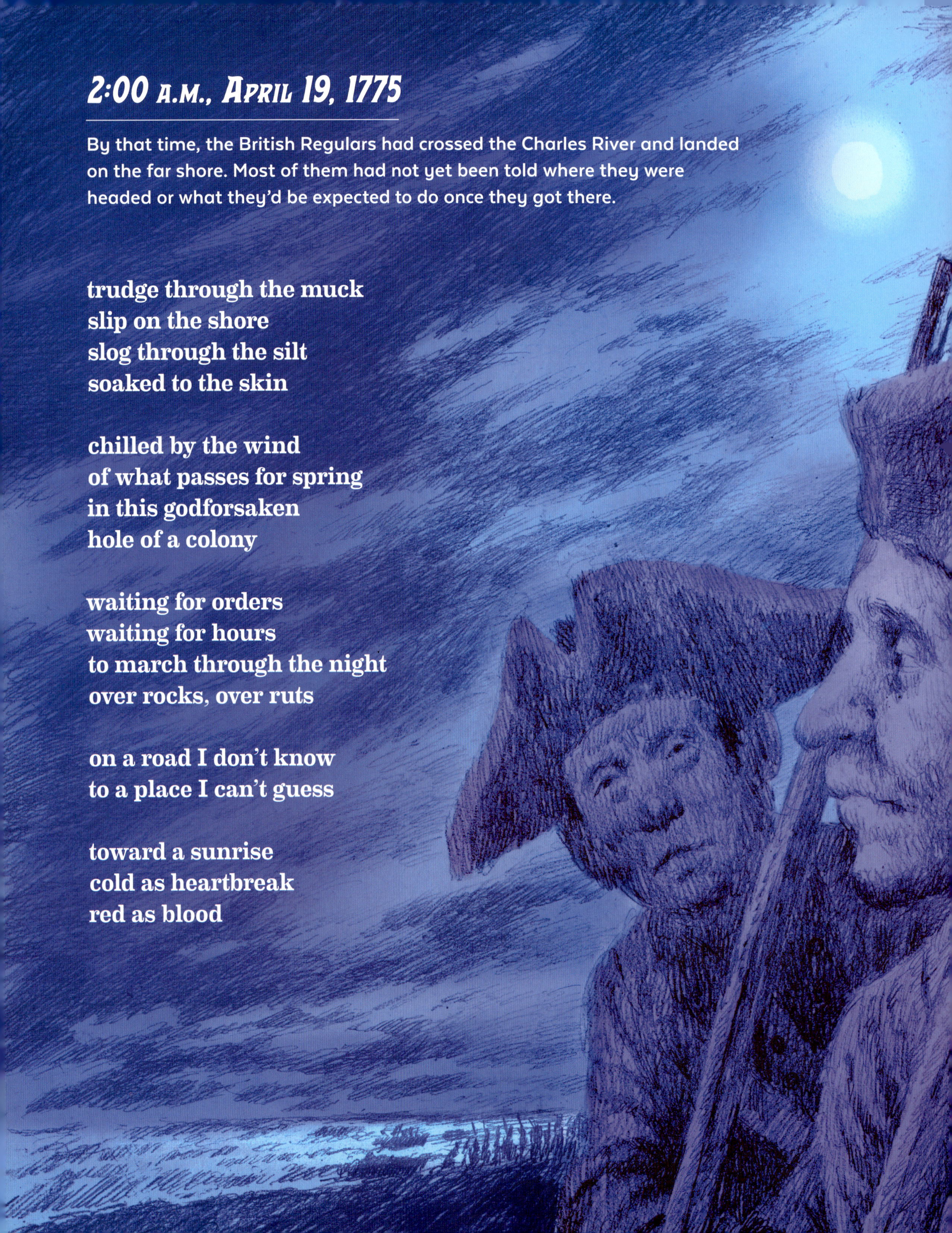

2:00 A.M., APRIL 19, 1775

By that time, the British Regulars had crossed the Charles River and landed on the far shore. Most of them had not yet been told where they were headed or what they'd be expected to do once they got there.

trudge through the muck
slip on the shore
slog through the silt
soaked to the skin

chilled by the wind
of what passes for spring
in this godforsaken
hole of a colony

waiting for orders
waiting for hours
to march through the night
over rocks, over ruts

on a road I don't know
to a place I can't guess

toward a sunrise
cold as heartbreak
red as blood

“Cold and disagreeable, a kind of second winter.”

—Lord Hugh Percy, letter describing spring in New England, 1775

AROUND 2:00 A.M., APRIL 19, 1775

The Regulars who stopped Revere, Dawes, and Prescott took Paul Revere prisoner. William Dawes escaped but lost his horse. Only Samuel Prescott kept on toward Concord, stopping here and there to warn people of the coming threat. In the town of Lincoln, he pounded on the door of a blacksmith's shop, waking two enslaved men inside.

sleep can loosen
any chain

can't put shackles
on a dream

but now blows hit the door
like a hammer on the anvil
voice raging hot
as fire in the forge

stealing the sleep
breaking the dream

shouting of freedom
that won't be for me

"Even an African, has Equally as good a right to his Liberty in common with Englishmen."

—Lemuel Haynes, "Liberty Further Extended: Or Free thoughts on the illegality of Slave-keeping," 1776

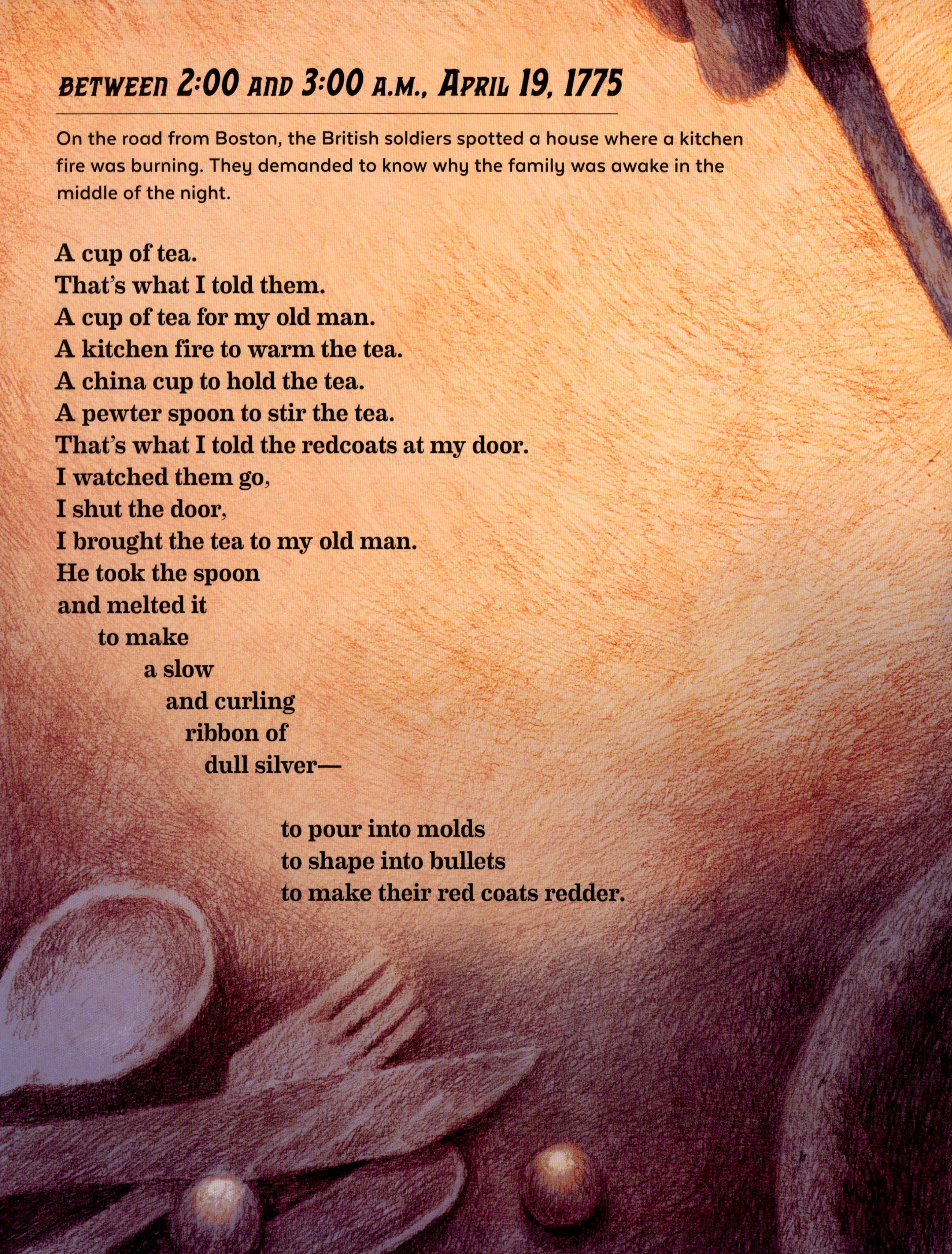

BETWEEN 2:00 AND 3:00 A.M., APRIL 19, 1775

On the road from Boston, the British soldiers spotted a house where a kitchen fire was burning. They demanded to know why the family was awake in the middle of the night.

A cup of tea.
That's what I told them.
A cup of tea for my old man.
A kitchen fire to warm the tea.
A china cup to hold the tea.
A pewter spoon to stir the tea.
That's what I told the redcoats at my door.
I watched them go,
I shut the door,
I brought the tea to my old man.
He took the spoon
and melted it
to make
a slow
and curling
ribbon of
dull silver—

to pour into molds
to shape into bullets
to make their red coats redder.

"You may depend upon it, that as the Rebels have now had time to prepare, they are determined to go through with it."
—Lord Hugh Percy, letter, 1775

Between 4:30 and 5:00 a.m., April 19, 1775

In Lexington, sixteen-year-old Jonathan Harrington was wakened by his mother. "Jonathan, get up! The Regulars are coming and something must be done!" she told him. With other armed men, Jonathan headed for the town green to confront the soldiers marching their way.

Give us a song, Jon
they say
and I do

but how I can give them
a spray of notes
a wisp of melody

how can I give them something
none of us can hold?

When that dawn breaks
my tunes float out
into the chill gray air,
carrying the captain's orders
to every soldier's ear:

Gather here   *Stay together*   *Stand fast*

and I hope I've given them something
all of us can hold.

"Captain Parker ... gave orders for every man to stand his ground."

—Corporal John Munroe, Lexington Militia, sworn statement, 1824

Who's Speaking?

The speakers of the poems all had some real-life connection to Paul Revere and his famous ride.

The Stable Boy: This boy, whose name we don't know, had heard from a friend that British officers were talking about a mission that night. Despite his speed, the boy wasn't first with the news. Revere told him, "You are the third person who has brought me the same information."

Dr. Warren's Informant: Dr. Warren was careful to keep the name of his informant a secret. It might have been someone close to General Gage, the royal governor of Massachusetts and commander of British forces in North America. Gage said that he had told only one other person his plans for a raid on Concord.

Robert Newman and **Captain John Pulling Jr.** climbed the steeple of Old North Church. Newman was the sexton, responsible for taking care of the building. That meant he had a key. Pulling was a vestryman, part of the group in charge of the church.

Reverend Mather Byles Jr.: The rector, or priest, of Old North Church (also called Christ Church) was loyal to King George III of England. That was one reason why, in the morning of April 18, 1775, the committee who governed the church asked him to leave. A year later, Byles and his family left for Canada, never to return.

Joshua Bentley, a boat builder, and **Thomas Richardson**, a shipwright, were the friends who rowed Revere across the Charles River, slipping right past a British warship.

John Larkin was a merchant. A family tradition says that the horse he lent Paul Revere was named Brown Beauty. Larkin never saw his mare again. She was taken by the British soldiers who captured Paul Revere.

Sergeant William Munroe went on to fight in the Revolution, eventually reaching the rank of colonel. After the war, he returned to run his family's tavern in Lexington.

Betty Clarke's father was known for supporting the colonists against the English government. Betty grew up with eleven brothers and sisters, and she lived all her life in her childhood home near Lexington Green.

Dr. Samuel Prescott: A doctor who made house calls, Prescott knew the roads and the country around Lexington and Concord well, which helped him evade British troops and make it all the way to his hometown of Concord. He later served as a surgeon and a privateer in the Revolutionary War. After being taken prisoner, he died in 1777, and never returned to marry his fiancée.

British Soldier: It wasn't an easy night for any of the Regulars. They were rowed across the Charles River in crowded boats, waded ashore through icy water, struggled through a marsh, and waited hours for orders and provisions before they even got started on an eighteen-mile march in the dark toward Concord.

Enslaved Servants: We do not know the names of the two enslaved men who were woken by Prescott. We do know that they alerted one of their enslavers, Mary Hartwell. She, or perhaps her husband, ran to share Prescott's warning with the captain of the local militia.

The Woman in the Kitchen: When soldiers pounded on her door, the woman who answered told them that she was up to make a cup of tea for her "old man," since he was sick. The soldiers never found out that the couple were actually melting down their pewter dishes to make bullets.

Jonathan Harrington: Just sixteen years old, Jonathan was a fife player in the Lexington Militia. A fifer, often a boy or a teenager, listened to a captain's orders and played tunes that everyone could hear, letting the soldiers know what to do. Jonathan was the youngest militia member on Lexington Green. He went on to serve in the army, survive the war, and live to age ninety-six.

The Battles of Lexington and Concord

As the British Regulars marched northwest from Boston, word of their approach spread from one Massachusetts town to another. Most of those towns had militias, bands of men (usually between sixteen and sixty years old) who had their own weapons and some military training.

At dawn, between seven and eight hundred Regulars arrived at Lexington. They were surprised to find themselves facing between seventy and eighty armed men—the Lexington Militia. No one is sure who fired the first shot, but shortly eight militia members were dead, one British soldier had been wounded, and the outnumbered militia was in retreat.

The Regulars continued on to Concord and came face-to-face with a larger militia at the North Bridge. This time it was the professional soldiers who were outnumbered and had to retreat.

Not far from Concord, the Regulars met a column of reinforcements under the command of Lord Hugh Percy. But they still didn't have enough men or ammunition to carry on the fight. "The rebels were in great numbers, the whole country having collected for twenty miles around," Lord Percy later wrote.

The British troops began a second retreat, keeping to the road. The militia members cut across fields and woods and hid behind hills, trees, buildings, and stone walls, attacking whenever they could. "There was not a stone-wall, or house . . . from whence the rebels did not fire upon us," wrote Lord Percy.

By sunset, when the exhausted Regulars made it back to Charlestown, 73 men had been killed and 174 injured. Nearly one hundred of the colonial militia were dead or wounded. But on the whole, the day was a startling success for the colonists and a humiliating loss for the Regulars.

It was also the start of the American Revolution.

What Happened to Paul Revere?

Paul Revere was captured by a small band of British soldiers not far from Lexington. But (as Revere pointed out to his captors) the countryside that night was a dangerous place for a few soldiers on their own. Revere's captors decided to free all of their prisoners so that they could get back quickly to the safety of the main force.

Without his horse, Paul Revere returned to Jonas Clarke's house, and then helped retrieve a trunk of valuable papers belonging to John Hancock from the Lexington tavern. As Revere and a companion carried the trunk away to stash in a nearby wood, they heard gunfire from the Lexington Green—the first shots of the American Revolution.

Didn't Paul Revere Shout, "The British Are Coming!"?

No, and for two very good reasons. First of all, he didn't shout because his mission was secret. Yelling in the streets would likely have gotten him arrested.

Second, Paul Revere *was* British. All colonists were. The American colonies were part of England. (The Declaration of Independence wasn't written or signed until 1776.) In 1775, most colonists, even those like Paul Revere, thought of themselves as standing up for their full rights as Englishmen.

Paul Revere's Life and Times

1715: Apollos Rivoire immigrated from France to Boston. He later changed his name to "Paul Rivoire" and then to "Paul Revere."

1734: On December 21, Paul Revere Sr. and Deborah Hitchborn Revere had a son, also named Paul. He was their third child.

1754: Paul Revere Sr. died. The younger Paul, at the age of nineteen, began to shoulder responsibility for his father's silversmith business.

1757: Paul Revere and Sarah Orne married.

1765: Paul Revere joined the Sons of Liberty.

1773: Sarah Revere died. Paul Revere likely helped to plan the Boston Tea Party. He rode from Boston to New York to spread word of this protest against the tax on tea. Paul Revere and Rachel Walker married.

1774: Paul Revere rode from Boston to Portsmouth, New Hampshire, to warn that British soldiers were planning to seize gunpowder held at a fort there.

1775: Paul Revere rode to spread the word of British soldiers marching from Boston toward Lexington and Concord. The American Revolution began.

1776: Paul Revere built a gunpowder mill to supply the Continental Army. He joined the Massachusetts Militia as a major (he was later promoted to lieutenant colonel) and was given command of Castle Island, a fortress in Boston Harbor.

1779: Paul Revere took part in a failed expedition to attack a British fort near Penobscot Bay (then in Massachusetts but now a part of Maine). He was accused of cowardice and refusal to obey orders on this mission.

1782: Paul Revere demanded a court martial and was cleared of all charges.

1783: The Revolutionary War ended. The United States became an independent country. Paul Revere opened a hardware store in Boston.

1788: Paul Revere opened a foundry where metal objects, including nails, bolts, cannons, and church bells, were cast.

1801: Paul Revere opened a mill to produce sheet copper.

1811: Paul Revere retired.

1813: Rachel Revere died.

1818: Paul Revere died at the age of eighty-three. He left behind a large family, including more than fifty grandchildren.

To Learn More

Books

- *And Then What Happened, Paul Revere?* by Jean Fritz, illustrated by Margot Tomes. New York: Puffin Books, 1973.
- *The Many Rides of Paul Revere* by James Cross Giblin. New York: Scholastic Press, 2007.
- "Paul Revere's Ride" by Henry Wadsworth Longfellow. This long poem is fiction, not history—but it's an exciting read! Take what you have learned about Paul Revere from this book and other nonfiction sources and compare it to how Longfellow told the story.

Places

Many locations connected with Paul Revere and his ride have been preserved for history. You can visit them in person or check out their websites for a virtual tour.

- The Freedom Trail (Boston, Massachusetts), thefreedomtrail.org
- Jonas Clarke's house (Lexington, Massachusetts), lexingtonhistory.org
- Minute Man National Historic Park and Battle Road (Massachusetts), nps.gov/mima/index.htm
- Old North Church (Boston, Massachusetts), oldnorth.com
- Paul Revere House (Boston, Massachusetts), paulreverehouse.org

Documents

- See a letter written by Paul Revere, describing his ride of April 18–19, 1775. masshist.org/database/viewer.php?item_id=99

Films

- "First Shot: The Day the Revolution Began" created by the Lexington Historical Society, 2009. youtube.com/watch?v=mB3WDa9RSK8
- "The Minute Men: Neighbors in Arms" created by Minute Man National Historic Park. nps.gov/mima/learn/historyculture/the-militia-and-minute-men-of-1775.htm

Selected Bibliography

Although this is partly a work of fiction, it's based upon extensive research, including the following resources. Works marked with an asterisk contain most of the essential quotations used in the book.

*Beyer, Rick. "First Shot: The Day the Revolution Began." Lexington Historical Society, 2009. youtube.com/watch?v=mB3WDa9RSK8.

*Bolton, Charles Knowles, ed. *Letters of Hugh, Earl Percy, from Boston and New York, 1774-1776*. Boston: Charles E. Goodspeed, 1902. 49, 53. Spelling modernized. loc.gov/resource/gdcmassbookdig.lettersofhughear01nort/?st=gallery.

*Fischer, David Hackett. *Paul Revere's Ride*. New York: Oxford University Press, 1994.

Kollen, Richard P. *The Patriot Parson of Lexington, Massachusetts: Reverend Jonas Clarke and the American Revolution*. Charleston, SC: The History Press, 2016.

Leehey, Patrick M. *What Was the Name of Paul Revere's Horse?* Boston: Paul Revere Memorial Association, 2019.

Minute Man National Historic Park. "The Militia and Minute Men of 1775." nps.gov/mima/learn/historyculture/the-militia-and-minute-men-of-1775.htm#:~:text=What%20was%20the%20militia%3F,men)%20commanded%20by%20a%20captain.

Old North Church. "History of Old North Church." oldnorth.com/our-history/.

———. "Why Do We Learn History?" January 18, 2022. Video, 4:22. oldnorth.com/our-history/.

*Revere, Paul. Letter to Jeremy Belknap, ca. 1798. Massachusetts Historical Society. masshist.org/database/viewer.php?item_id=99.

To everyone who believes democracy is worth fighting for —SLT

For my dad —NH

Acknowledgments

Many thanks to Tegan Kehoe and the experts at the Paul Revere Memorial Association, Emily Spence of Old North Illuminated, Sam McGinty at the Colonial Williamsburg Foundation, and Kate Criscitiello of the Lexington Historical Society for their time, generosity, and expertise.

Calkins Creek
An imprint of Astra Books for Young Readers,
a division of Astra Publishing House
astrapublishinghouse.com
Printed in China

ISBN: 978-1-6626-8138-7 (hc)
ISBN: 978-1-6626-8139-4 (eBook)
Library of Congress Control Number: 2025935706

First edition

10 9 8 7 6 5 4 3 2 1

Design by Barbara Grzeslo and Michelle Mayhall
The text is set in Eames Century Modern and Texta Alt.
The titles are set in Citrus Gothic Rough, Stranger, and hand-lettered.
The illustrations are done with graphite and colored digitally.